Advocacy in Action

by the same authors

Introducing Advocacy
The First Book of Speaking Up: A Plain Text Guide to Advocacy
ISBN 978 1 84310 475 9

Rules and Standards
The Second Book of Speaking Up: A Plain Text Guide to Advocacy
ISBN 978 1 84310 476 6

Listen Up! Speak Up!
The Third Book of Speaking Up: A Plain Text Guide to Advocacy
ISBN 978 1 84310 477 3

of related interest

Advocacy and Learning Disability
Edited by Barry Gray and Robin Jackson
ISBN 978 1 85302 942 4

Exploring Experiences of Advocacy by People with Learning Disabilities
Testimonies of Resistance
Edited by Duncan Mitchell, Rannveig Traustadottir, Rohhss Chapman, Louise
Townson, Nigel Ingham and Sue Ledger
ISBN 978 1 84310 359 2

Advocacy Skills for Health and Social Care Professionals
Neil Bateman
ISBN 978 1 85302 865 6

ISPEEK at Home
Over 1300 Visual Communication Images
Janet Dixon
ISBN 978 1 84310 510 7

ISPEEK at School
Over 1300 Visual Communication Images
Janet Dixon
ISBN 978 1 84310 511 4

Advocacy in Action

The Fourth Book of Speaking Up:
A Plain Text Guide to Advocacy

John Tufail and Kate Lyon

Jessica Kingsley Publishers
London and Philadelphia

First published in New Zealand in 2005
by People's Advocacy Network

This edition first published in 2007
by Jessica Kingsley Publishers
116 Pentonville Road
London N1 9JB, UK
and
400 Market Street, Suite 400
Philadelphia, PA 19106, USA

www.jkp.com

Library of Congress Cataloging in Publication Data
A CIP catalog record for this book is available from the Library of Congress

British Library Cataloguing in Publication Data
A CIP catalogue record for this book is available from the British Library

ISBN 978 1 84310 478 0

Printed and bound in the People's Republic of China
by Nanjing Amity Printing
APC-FT4808-4

'To teach a man how he may learn
to grow independently, and for himself,
is the greatest service
that one man can do another.'
Benjamin Jowett

Contents

1. Introduction

This is the **fourth book of speaking up**. The first three books looked at what advocacy is and the things you need to know in order to start out as an advocate. In this book we hope you can learn what it is like to BE an advocate.

We will start off with another story. Then we will use this story to look at an important part of advocacy – how to PLAN.

We will then look at some of the types of problems that advocates might have to deal with. And we will talk about some of the problems advocates might have to face.

If you haven't done any advocacy before, or you don't feel very confident about speaking up, it might be a good idea if you look at the first three books before you read this book.

Advocacy means working with people with lots of different types of problems – helping people solve their problems, giving them the confidence to speak up for themselves. Most of the problems that people you will be working with will have happened because other people don't understand or don't listen.

Dilly's problems were mainly caused because people didn't listen to her properly.

2. Dilly's Story

When Dilly was nine she was in a car crash. Her legs were broken. Her hips were badly damaged. Her skull was fractured and her brain was damaged. She spent a long time in hospital. 'She'll never get better,' the doctors said.

Dilly spent ten years in a special hospital. Then the government decided the hospital should close. 'People like Dilly should live in the community,' said the government. 'It will be better for them.'

So Dilly was moved into a special home. She lived in this home with three other people whose brains were damaged. Who couldn't walk very well. Who needed medication. There were people there to help Dilly and her housemates because they couldn't manage alone. These helpers were called support workers.

Dilly had difficulty speaking and couldn't say words properly. She also had a problem with one of her legs. This meant she had to wear a special type of boot and couldn't walk very far.

The doctors said that Dilly had bad epilepsy and had to take a lot of medication. Other doctors said that Dilly had been so badly damaged that she couldn't really understand things or work things out. Other people would have to make decisions for her. So they did.

They decided what she would eat. They decided what she would wear. They decided where she would go and what she would do when she got there. They decided what time she would go to bed and get up. They decided what television programmes she would watch and what music she would listen to.

The three other people in the house complained about Dilly. The support workers complained too. They all said that Dilly kept losing her temper. She would tear up magazines. She would switch off the television and shout at people.

A doctor came and gave Dilly some medication to calm her down. 'Dilly must take this medicine three times a day,' the Doctor said. 'If she doesn't get better, I'll give her something stronger.'

And he did.

There were people who would come and try to teach Dilly things. 'Dilly can't concentrate,' they said. 'Sometimes she falls asleep for no reason. Sometimes she throws things about in a temper. We can't teach her anything.'

When Dilly went to the day centre, she would tear up the art paper and shout at the staff. Then she would fall asleep at the table.

Because Dilly was a problem, she never went out except to go to the day centre or to a special swimming pool for therapy.

Dilly's father would visit her about once a month. He was told it would be best not to take her out because she might cause a problem, or have a fit. He

used to take her into the garden and talk with her. He told the people looking after Dilly that the reason that she was causing problems was because she was unhappy.

'She can't be unhappy, she has everything she needs,' they said. 'She has lots of support, everyone is kind to her. 'We've tried everything.'

There was a big meeting.

'Dilly can't stay here,' said the support workers.

'Dilly can't come to the day centre any more,' said the day centre workers.

'Dilly has to go to a special home for people with bad tempers,' everyone said. 'She needs a lot of support.'

Dilly's father was at the meeting.

'I'm unhappy that Dilly isn't here,' he said. 'I don't think it is right that you talk about her future unless she is here. I don't like this meeting.'

The other people at the meeting said that Dilly couldn't understand. They said she would shout and stop the meeting.

'We have to decide for her,' they said. 'You can speak for Dilly. You are her father.'

'I'm speaking for Dilly now,' said the father.

'We didn't mean that,' they said. 'We meant that you have to listen to us and do what is best for Dilly. What we decide will be best for Dilly.'

'I want this meeting to stop now,' said the father. 'I want to get some advice, I think you are all wrong about Dilly.'

So the meeting was stopped.

Dilly's father contacted an advocacy organisation and explained the problem. He said he felt helpless because he didn't know enough to argue with the professionals. 'But I know that I can understand Dilly and she can understand me,' he explained.

'Nobody will let me see Dilly's records. They say they are Dilly's and no-one else can see them,' he said. 'They treat me as if I wouldn't understand them anyway.'

The advocate and Dilly's father wrote down all the things that he was worried about. They wrote down all the things that might be done to help Dilly. They met with Dilly and explained what they were going to do. Dilly seemed to understand. She seemed happy.

The advocate explained that Dilly's father had a right to see Dilly's records. She explained that Dilly had a right to ask other doctors for their opinion, and that Dilly's father could do this for her.

Together, the advocate and Dilly's father wrote a lot of letters. They were allowed to see Dilly's records.

They saw that Dilly had only had four epileptic fits in five years but her medication was very high. And they saw that nobody had properly assessed Dilly's needs and abilities for a long, long time. So they asked another doctor to look at Dilly.

This doctor said that Dilly was overmedicated. She said she thought the father was right and that Dilly could understand a lot of things. She said that Dilly had not been properly examined for about ten years. She thought that the reason Dilly fell asleep and couldn't concentrate was because she was given too much medicine.

The new doctor asked a psychologist to look at Dilly.

The psychologist said that he thought that the main reason that Dilly got so angry was because nobody was trying to understand her and listen to her.

The psychologist asked a speech therapist to work with Dilly.

The speech therapist said that if people treated Dilly with dignity and patience, Dilly could communicate.

But...

other people would have to take the time to learn Dilly's special ways of communicating.

After a while, all these people – the new doctor, the psychologist, the speech therapist and some others – agreed that Dilly could understand a lot. 'Other people should learn how Dilly says things,' they said. 'The medication is a big part of the problem.' People have to live with Dilly's epilepsy, it is not that dangerous, the medication must be cut down a lot.'

Dilly improved a lot. She still gets angry sometimes, but people know why. They can understand her. For example, they now understand that when she got angry at the day centre it was because she didn't like being given a big piece of paper and some paint and then left alone every day!

Even though Dilly's medication was cut down a lot, Dilly still hardly ever has epileptic fits.

 Dilly goes out a lot now. She goes to concerts. She goes to a leisure centre and does exercises. She goes shopping with her support worker.

Dilly doesn't get angry and destroy things. She laughs a lot and is popular. She plays music and sings a lot. She goes out with her father. She even goes on holiday with him sometimes.

But most importantly, people treat Dilly with respect and understanding – because, with her father, she has learned to speak up.

3. Making a Plan

Dilly and her advocate had to work very hard to achieve what they did. But they couldn't have achieved anything if they hadn't sat down together and worked out a plan about how they were going to work together and what it was exactly that Dilly wanted.

Everyone makes plans.

For example, when you wake up in the morning you plan what clothes you are going to wear. You plan the order you are going to put them on. If you don't, you might end up putting your underpants on after your trousers. Like Superman.

Or not!

The point is that you are so used to planning things that most of the time you don't realise you are doing it. But sometimes you do things you haven't done before. Then you have to think about how you are going to do it. You have to plan it.

Like going on a picnic. You have to plan lots of things:

- where you are going

- what day and time you are going

- how you are going to get there

- what you are going to eat and drink

- what you are going to carry everything in

- who is going to carry it

- how much money you will need...and so on.

Planning a picnic is complicated!

Advocates and their partners have to make plans.

Plans are necessary for three reasons:

- They remind you of what it is you want to achieve – your goal.

- They help you remember all the things that you have to do in order to get there.

- They help you get everything in the right order.

It's OK making a plan in your head if you are doing something simple, like getting dressed, or if you are doing something where it doesn't matter too much if you get things a bit wrong, like planning a picnic. But the things the advocate and the partner will be planning are going to be important. You have to do everything right. You don't want to forget things. You want to get everything in the right order.

The first thing you need to do in order to start planning is to be quite sure you know exactly what it is you want.

It's no use saying, 'I'm not very happy and I want something done about it!' You need to be able to say exactly why you're not happy and what it is you want done about it! This might not be as easy as you think!

nyah nyah nyah nyah nyah!!!!

For example, say you live in a flat and every time you go out the same children call you names and throw things at you.

Because you're different. You go to an advocate and say, 'I can't live here any more! I want to move!'

You see! You know what the problem is! And you think that the only thing you can do about it is to go away, leave the problem behind.

But the same thing might happen when you get to your new place. And anyway, why should you have to move from YOUR home – you haven't done anything wrong! You have a right to live where you want and be safe from abuse.

What has happened here is that you have confused two things. You have identified the problem. That's fine, it's the ignorant people who abuse you. But you just thought that YOU are the problem! You think that YOU have to move so you don't get abused.

Is that right? Will it solve your problem? Of course it won't!

So...
just thinking about a plan helps you think about what exactly it is you want to achieve. You don't really WANT to move. You just thought you HAD to move. There's a difference. What you want is to stop being abused.

Once you have sorted out what it is you really want, you can go to the next stage of planning. That is, you can make up a list of all the different ways you can achieve what you want. You can put them in order.

So you might decide that the best way to deal with your problem is just to persuade the children to stop abusing you. You can think of different ways this can be done. You and your advocate could approach the children's parents. After all, they might not know what's been going on.

You might decide that the children are abusing you because they are afraid of you because you are different. You might think it a good idea to talk to the school that the children go to so they can teach the children not to be afraid of people who seem different. Maybe even have someone from a self-advocacy group talking to the children.

You will come up with a lot of different things you can do. You will probably find that leaving your home comes bottom of the list!

When you are quite sure you know exactly what it is you want, you should record it in some way.

This will help you if things get a bit confused later on. When you have recorded everything it will be easier to decide which things are very important and which are not. It will be easier to decide the best order in which things are done. It will be easier to work out who best to talk to about things and the things you need to find out about.

Some people draw their plans on a big chart. This allows them to see things more clearly.

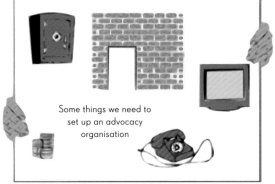

Some things we need to set up an advocacy organisation

Some people who find it hard to read make videos of their plans. They can watch themselves and other people talking about their plans whenever they want.

This helps them remember the important things that need doing.

This reminds them of what they want most of all.

4. Advocacy Problems

We have already looked at some of the problems that you might face as an advocate. For example, in the **second book of speaking up** we looked at conflicts of interest and duty of care. We have also thought about confidentiality and privacy and some of the problems these issues raise. But there are many other problems that advocates face.

Some of these problems you might come across quite often. Others might never happen to you – if you are lucky...or careful.

The thing to remember about problems though is to remember that everyone has them. They are part of life. And they are part of learning.

So there is always a good thing about problems – no matter how bad they might seem. Problems are like good teachers – they make you think.

Even if you make a mistake in trying to solve a problem, you can learn from that mistake. It will give you the chance to get it right next time. The only people who don't make mistakes are people who give their problems to other people to solve...

Oops! Isn't that a mistake a lot of the time?

If you want to be in charge of your own life you should always want to try to solve your own problems. But often it's best to try to solve them with support from other people. In the end though it should be YOU who makes the choice about what is the right answer to the problem.

So let's look at some of the kinds of problems you might come across as an advocate.

Dependency

The most common problem that any advocate faces is how to prevent the advocacy partner becoming too dependent on the advocate. After all, the advocate is usually working with someone who has probably never been allowed to make even simple decisions before.

Becoming independent, making your own choices, speaking up for yourself can all be quite a frightening experience for such a person.

It is important that right from the beginning the advocate makes it clear to the partner that advocates are not there to make the partner's decisions. Not there to tell the partner what choices to make.

Otherwise all that will happen is that the partner will end up moving from one type of dependency into another. The partner will never learn to become independent. Will never learn to make real decisions and choices. Never learn the importance of being responsible for oneself and for others.

So it is important that the advocate is always consistent about the advocate's role AND the responsibilities of the partner.

For example, a partner faced with a lot of different choices about a big event says: 'I don't know what to do! Please tell me what to do.' The advocate would be very tempted

to 'help the partner out' by saying: 'I think you should do this.'

But this is not advocacy. This is advice.

And the problem is that the partner has always been given advice. Too much advice. Too many times! That's why the partner is so afraid to make a decision.

What an advocate should do is to sit with the partner and go through all the choices and let the partner work out what the consequences of each choice will be.

Remember for every choice made there will be a consequence. A consequence means that something will happen because of something you have done. If you make the right choice, the  consequence will be good. If you make the wrong choice the consequence will not be as good.

For example, there might be consequences about money. If you spend all your money on one thing (say food) you might not have enough left for something else you need (like transport).

Or you might be deciding about whether to take or not take a particular kind of medicine. You will need to know lots of things before you can make a proper choice – How necessary is the medicine for your health and safety? Will NOT taking it cause you harm? What are the side-effects of the medicine? Are there other medicines or forms of treatment that might be better for you?

Then when the partner really understands – and has all the information needed to make an **informed choice** – only the partner can decide what's the right thing to do. The advocate supports the partner in coming to a

decision. The advocate then respects this decision.

Advocacy is about helping people help themselves. It's about making people stronger – able to speak up for themselves.

So it's really important that the advocate works in a way that helps the partner grow in confidence, pride and dignity. This can only happen if the advocate works with the partner in such a way that the partner learns to grow into becoming independent to the best of his or her ability.

Remember in the **first book of speaking up** we agreed that the best advocate is one that works so well with the partner that after a while the advocate won't be needed any more? But we have seen that sometimes this is difficult.

Sometimes the partner becomes dependent on the advocate. The partner is so used to being dependent on other people that it is hard not to see the advocate as another person to be dependent on. But this is just swapping one type of dependency for another. It is not helping the partner to be strong and independent.

This is not good.

It is not good for the partner. It is not good for the advocate.

There are some simple rules that will help the advocate and the partner think about why this sort of thing should not happen, and how important it is. These have been talked about in earlier books, but it would be a good idea if we quickly look at them again:

- Advocates should always explain to the partner AND to all other parties that an advocate's main job is to help partners speak up for themselves.

- Advocates should always encourage the partner to take the lead in what they do together. This means the partner should, as much as possible, be the one who communicates with others. The advocate should only take the lead when absolutely necessary.

- Advocates and their partners should set clear boundaries about their relationships. They should have clear objectives about what they and the partner are trying to achieve. For example, advocates should be very careful about giving or taking presents. This is because it might confuse the way the partner thinks about the advocate. It might make the partner feel more dependent on the advocate.

- Advocates should not advise the partner which is the best choice to make or instruct the partner not to take a particular choice of action. The advocate should always help the partner understand ALL the choices available and the possible consequences of each action.

- Advocates and their partners should work out a clear plan about how they are going to achieve their objectives. Like Dilly and her father did with the advocate.

- An advocate should always try to make sure that the choices partners make are their own. They should work hard with the partner to make sure the decision has not been made because others have been bullying the partner to make a decision THEY want. Advocates should work with partners so they understand that decisions made just to please someone else are not usually good decisions.

Now, it is important that you understand that these guidelines are not hard-and-fast rules. For example, there might be times when it would be right to exchange gifts. It might help create trust and confidence – help build the partner's self-esteem. This is often the case in citizen advocacy when the advocate partner relationship is long-term and particularly close.

There will be times when the partner is not able to make an informed choice and the advocate has to make the right choice. You saw how this can happen when we talked about non-directed advocacy in the **first book of speaking up**. Advocates have to think as though they are in the same position as their partners and make the choice that the partners would make if they were well enough.

Remember – just being there is often enough to help the partner feel strong enough to speak up. You don't even have to be there in person.

Sometimes it might be best to encourage a person to go to a meeting on their own. This is a part of learning to be strong for yourself and in yourself.

In cases like this, just knowing that you COULD be there might be all that is needed.

Loyalty

Another common problem an advocate might face is when the advocate's loyalty to the partner is challenged.

The advocate should always be on the side of the partner – the person the advocate is speaking up with. But sometimes things occur that might make this difficult. This can happen in a number of ways.

1.   The advocate might begin to think the partner is being 'unreasonable' about something. So, the advocate, being a very 'reasonable' person, might try to convince the partner to change some of the things the partner is trying to say.

But...

as soon as advocates start doing this they stop being an advocate. The whole relationship is changed and the advocate becomes just one more person the partner can't trust and has to fight with.

2.   The advocate might be called a troublemaker or do-gooder. This might upset the advocate – especially if the words come from people the advocate respects or is a bit frightened of.

     This might make the advocate start to look for ways to look better so other people 'respect' the advocate more. This can mean that the advocate will start putting his or her own needs before the needs of the partner.

3. Sometimes a service provider might contact the advocate 'in private' to try to discuss a problem. The service provider might try to persuade the advocate that it would be best if the conversation was so private that it should be kept from the partner.

Often the person contacting the advocate in this way might say that it would be 'unprofessional' of the advocate to tell the partner anything and that it would be breaking a trust. 'If I can't trust you to keep this between us, how can I possibly work with you on a professional basis?' the service provider might say.

'They think I can't talk!'

Or he or she might say something like: 'It would be best if you don't discuss this with your partner. It might cause them a lot of distress. You don't want to do that, do you?'

But an advocate should never do this kind of thing. If the advocate keeps things from the partner that are about the partner, it is never a good thing. It means that you are keeping information from your partners that might stop them making choices and decisions that are right for them.

In fact, the advocate is making decisions for the partner. **This is not advocacy.**

4. Health professionals might approach an advocate and say that advocating for a particular person is dangerous because the person is making the wrong choices.

    For example, a partner might want to stop taking a particular medication and try something else. The doctor tells the advocate, 'If this person insists, through you, that the medication is changed, I will have to stop the medication completely because in my opinion it is the only medicine that will work. It will be your fault if the person gets really ill! You will be personally responsible for putting your partner at risk.'

'I do have a voice it's about ME!'

    This happens quite a lot. The advocate has to understand that this is very unethical behaviour by the doctor. It is like blackmail.

The advocate has to make it very clear to the doctor that the advocate's job is to help the partner understand all the choices and possible consequences, and then speak up for the partner.

The advocate cannot try to persuade the partner for or against any particular action. That is the doctor's job (or the caregiver's job, the social worker's job...). They are the experts.

5. Often an advocate might privately think that a partner is making the 'wrong' choice – and then will be told by someone that the reason the person is making the wrong choice is because of the advocate.
    Some advocates might want to tell that person that they don't agree with the choice the partner is making. But doing this will stop the advocate speaking up effectively for the partner.

6. An advocate might be speaking up for someone who doesn't like the services being provided by their service provider. But the service provider is also giving money

to the advocacy organisation that the advocate is working for!

The advocate's boss might say, 'Be careful, because we don't want to lose our funding. Don't do anything to upset the service provider. If you do, we won't have enough money to pay you!'

This is a BIG conflict of interest. It is one that happens quite a bit.

This is why an Advocacy Charter should always say it is important that advocacy organisations must always be independent.

These are just some of the ways in which the advocate's loyalty to the partner can be put at risk. Sometimes it is very hard to keep loyalty. You might want to look at the **second book of speaking up**, where we talk about duty of care and risk management, to see other examples of situations where an advocate's loyalty to the partner might be challenged.

5. Letting Go

The best thing an advocate can ever hear from the partner is: 'Thanks. You've been really helpful...but I don't need you any more!'

This is when all advocates know that they have done the best job that can be done.

But a lot of the time this doesn't happen. Sometimes partners will never feel confident enough to do things alone. They become so comfortable having an advocate around that they don't really want to let go.

We looked at this earlier so you know how important it is. It is about the partner becoming too dependent on the advocate.

Even though YOU can see that they will be OK to make decisions on their own, find out things on their own, go to meetings on their own, the partner can't see it – can't see that it would be better for them.

But if the partner can't experience making their own choices without an advocate around, it will be difficult for them ever to be truly themselves, truly independent.

The advocate must always be prepared to say to the partner that the time has come to let go, to let the partner go their own way.

This can be very hard, and the partner has to be prepared for this to happen. You don't just say, 'Bye, bye, nice to have met you, you're on your own now.' Like everything else the advocate and partner do together, letting go has to be planned, has to be discussed. The partner has to understand that it is necessary.

Before you let the partner go, you have to be sure that the partner is going to be supported in other ways – so that all the things learned won't be lost. Each situation is different, so there are a lot of different ways this can be done.

Sometimes it might be a good idea to have a meeting with the partner and some friends – maybe a support worker or someone from work, or a place of worship, or members of the family.

One of the best ways is to make sure that those advocacy partners who want to become self-advocates join a Speaking Up group – or start one if there isn't one around they feel comfortable with. There's nothing wrong with an advocate helping a partner do this.

So, if you do things right, explain to the partner and always encourage independence and self-advocacy, you will be giving more and more control to the partner. Partners can then understand that letting go of this special relationship is a big step but they want to be learning how to do things for themselves and by themselves.

Sometimes partners might tell people that they need to make decisions alone and ask people not to get worried about things – to give them space to grow.

Sometimes partners just want to be sure that someone will be there if things need talking over or help is needed in finding things out. Part of the letting-go process might be for the advocate to see the partner after, say, six months – to see how things are going. This might help give the partner confidence.

The main thing is, that letting go should always be seen as a good thing – something to be happy and proud about.

Letting go doesn't always mean that you are not going to see the partner again. For example, you might be a person's advocate because you are part of the same self-advocacy project.

What it does mean though is that you have both agreed that your value as an advocate has come to an end because partners become strong enough to speak up for themselves.

So, if seeing your ex-partner again is necessary – especially if you see your ex-partner fairly often – part of the letting go may be to give a few words of encouragement when you meet. You might even want to ask ex-partners for advice about something – so they can see that you respect their judgement and ability to make the right choices. This will help them make right choices for themselves.

6. Advocacy and Conflict

As we saw in the **third book of speaking up**, good advocacy should aim to reduce conflict wherever possible. Good advocates, in fact, will help their partners think ahead so that problems can be seen before they become too big and urgent. But sometimes there will be conflict and sometimes people will not understand what advocacy is about.

This chapter will give you some idea of the sort of problems that might lead to conflict. You will see that the best way of getting rid of these problems is to think ahead and make sure that everyone understands exactly what an advocate does and how an advocate can help.

Many conflicts involving advocacy happen when someone doesn't understand what the advocate's job is, or how the advocate can help. Here are some examples:

- A social worker accuses an advocate of supporting 'unrealistic' demands by the partner and threatens to complain to the advocate's funders.

- Caregivers might get angry with an advocate because they think the advocate should help the partner understand 'what's best' for the partner from the caregiver's point of view.

- Care professionals stop an advocate from attending meetings with the partner because 'it is not appropriate for reasons of confidentiality'.

- A doctor refuses to discuss the partner's medical condition with the advocate – even though the partner has given verbal permission for this to happen.

- The manager of a residential home refuses to allow an advocate access on the grounds that the advocate might cause trouble and upset staff and residents.

- A caregiver complains that an advocate's partner is getting better services than her child because of the advocate. She says that this is unfair and that everyone should get the same.

- An employer will not allow an advocate to attend a job interview with the partner.

If you look at all the above examples again, you will see that in each case the conflict has arisen because either:

(a) somebody has completely misunderstood what the role of an advocate is

or

(b) somebody has misunderstood the right of partners to have advocates speak up for them. They think the advocate is acting like a lawyer.

It is important that the advocate's role (and the partner's right to have an advocate) is explained to EVERYBODY who is likely to be involved in the partner's care and the provision of services.

An example – let's look at the employer who said that the advocate can't be at the interview. Why might the employer have refused to allow an advocate to be present?

Employers might think that an interview might be a waste of time with an advocate present. The advocate would be in the way. It would stop employers getting to know the person they might want to employ. The employer might think the advocate will become a barrier instead of a help.

This seems quite reasonable really. But if the advocate and partner had written to the employer when first applying for the job and clearly explained the role of the advocate, the benefit of having the advocate present, then maybe the employer would have behaved differently.

The example of the doctor refusing to give confidential medical information to an advocate is different. Here the doctor might have different things on his mind:

First, there is a tradition in Western medicine that medical information is too complicated and potentially dangerous to share with a patient or anyone who has not been given medical training.

Personal File

But...

this is changing as governments have realised that patients should be seen as equal partners with doctors and others in their own health care and that **people have a right to access their own medical records** and be told everything they want to know about their health and social care.

Second, there are strict laws about sharing confidential information with other people. The doctor might have been worried about breaking one of these laws.

But...

the doctor may not have understood that **the advocate has as much right to the information as the patient – because the patient has actually given him that right**.

If a partner can't write, then someone else can write or record the permission for them – making sure that the way this is done is in a way that the doctor is sure that this is what the partner wants.

So knowing your rights and communicating properly can stop a lot of conflict. It's important when you are advocating that you don't just think that everyone will know what an advocate does and what an advocate's rights are.

Play safe and make sure that people REALLY know what an advocate's rights are.

Of course these aren't the only times that an advocate will come across conflict. Sometimes you will have conflict with your partner. This often happens when the partner is upset or confused about something.

For example, you might have to give your partner some bad news. This might make any partner angry – so they might take their anger out on you.

Again, you will be the best person to know how to deal with it. But here are some general hints that might help you:

- If partners seem confused and you do not think they will be able to think properly, just make sure that they are safe and not likely to cause harm to themselves or others. Then politely withdraw until they have had time to calm down.

- Don't be judgemental or shout back. Remember, everyone gets angry at times – often with the wrong person! Even if your partner is abusive to you, keep calm and remain polite.

- Be careful not to say anything that your partner might think of as threatening, like: 'If you carry on like this I will stop being your partner.' Even if you think the relationship is breaking down and you might have to end the relationship, saying it in the middle of a row is not a good idea!

Sometimes your partner might get angry in a meeting. When this happens, it is important not to seem to be supporting the people who your partner is getting angry with. Don't say something like, 'I'm sorry my partner is shouting at you.' Instead, just ask for a break for your partner. Stop the meeting and only return when your partner is ready.

Finally, two important things to remember.

First, one of the worst things an advocate can do is to make promises that can't be kept.

Like saying, 'Yes, we will definitely get you the money to go on an overseas holiday.' This is bad advocacy and can do a lot of harm. You should always try to be realistic about what you and your partner can achieve together.

You should explain that even if you do not achieve everything together, the fact that you have done your best and done it right is a good thing in itself. It's a good learning experience.

Second, even though you try not to make mistakes – you will make them. Just don't be afraid of making mistakes – and try to learn from them!

7. Advocacy and Communication

What is communication?

Well, most people think that communication is about writing and speaking. And about watching and listening to the television and radio. And that's it... But it isn't.

Communication is about understanding.

Not everyone communicates in the same way. Just because most people can make themselves clear in spoken language doesn't mean that people who can't 'speak' like that can't communicate.

EVERYONE can communicate. Even someone who can't speak at all can communicate. Trouble is, because most people don't have to think about communicating, they get a bit lazy when communicating is hard.

People tend to blame others when they can't understand them.

People get a bit impatient and don't watch and listen properly. Remember?... We talked about this in the **third book of speaking up.**

Communicating with patience, courtesy and understanding is really important in advocacy.

It is particularly important when you are trying to understand someone who can't communicate in ordinary speech and can't use a sign language. Not only do you have to be sure that you can read the type of language that your partner is using (this might be just using head and body movements and some non-verbal sounds, for example), but you also have to

convince other people that you can understand properly. Otherwise people might think that you are just advocating for what you think your partner's needs are – instead of for what your partner thinks is needed.

And remember we talked earlier about how people not understanding about advocacy can cause problems? And how those problems can make people angry? This is why communicating with everyone involved in your partner's needs is so important.

And always try to use the RIGHT way to communicate, because these days there are many ways of communicating. If you are not actually communicating face-to-face you can:

- communicate by
  telephone, letter, e-mail
  or fax

- set up conferences
  through a computer

- record information on video or
  minicam

- use Braille or signing

- record information in an audio-cassette and send it
  by post

- write information in a brochure or a leaflet and post it, hand it out or leave it in places like libraries, community centres, schools, doctors' surgeries etc. for people to read and learn.

It is important that you always use the best way of communicating in a given situation.

It's no use sending a long complicated letter to someone who is not going to be able to read it – or understand it.

Even if you know that there might be someone who can help a person understand what you are saying, it would be better if you could think of a way of communicating in a way that doesn't need to be 'translated'. Like recording your message on a cassette instead of on paper, or using pictures instead of, or as well as, words.

Some things we need to set up an advocacy organisation

Another important thing about good communication is making sure that you are communicating with the right people!

For example, say your advocacy partner is living in a residential home. She comes to you and says that she is a vegetarian but she is being made to eat meat. There are a lot of people you could contact to raise this matter:

- the person who makes the food

- the person responsible for the Personal Care Plan

- the home manager

- the home manager's boss

- the partner's social worker

- the people responsible for paying for your advocacy partner's services.

What the advocate will do in such a situation is to talk with the partner and decide which of these people is the best person to contact to solve the problem as quickly and with as little fuss as possible. You would want to contact someone with:

- direct knowledge of the situation

- the authority to do something about it.

So you would probably not want to contact the person who actually prepared the food, because that person probably wouldn't have the authority to change things. And you would probably not want to contact the manager's boss (at least not at first!), because that person might not know enough about the situation.

In this case, the best person to contact at first might be the home manager – because that is the person who would have all the facts and has the authority to make immediate changes. Only if the manager can't or won't help would you want to contact the manager's boss or any of the other people on the list.

However, what you might want to do is, if the changes that your partner wants are made, let ALL the other people on the list know that these changes have been made – and why they have been made.

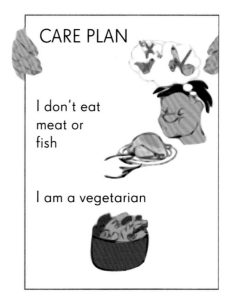

CARE PLAN

I don't eat meat or fish

I am a vegetarian

You would want the changes recorded on the partner's Personal Care Plan as well. You and your partner would do this by asking for a care planning meeting so that everyone involved in providing services for the partner could agree to the changes together.

8. Advocacy and the Law

Advocates are not lawyers. But the law is very important in advocacy. This is because the partner's rights and interests are protected by law. People with disability have a lot of rights that are set down by the law.

For example, in most countries these days the law says that what a person with disabilities receives depends on what each person's needs are, NOT on what is available or what service providers have available.

So, for example, if it can be clearly shown that a person needs a wheelchair, it is actually against the law for a service provider to say 'You can't have a wheelchair because we don't have one spare' or 'We think this person doesn't need a wheelchair, because he doesn't need to go out'.

Another example – people have a right to go on holiday. They also have a right to have a say in where they go on holiday and when! However, until recently, many service providers just arranged a holiday for people without asking them where and when they want to go! So people would be just packed into a coach and sent on holiday whether they liked it or not!

Advocates need to know that these things are wrong, that service providers can't do things like this any more! So you might think that only people who are trained to know a lot about the law can be advocates.

Well, of course it would be nice if all advocates knew everything there is to know about all the laws that affect their partners – but if that were the case, all advocates would be lawyers! And many people who would be good advocates would be put off from becoming advocates.

In fact, an advocate doesn't need to know any more about the law than their partner. All they need to know is how to find out what bit of law affects a particular need at a particular time. This is something that the advocate and the partner can do together so both can learn as they go along.

The advocate needs to learn the best ways of finding things out so these things can be shared with the partner.

Here is another story.

Mandy's story

Mandy lived in a residential home with four other people. It was a nice home, with nice gardens, and the staff were kind and helpful.

Mandy had her own room with her own TV and her own radio and CD player. She was really happy most of the time – except...she couldn't go to the shops on her own. She couldn't go out to meet friends on her own. She couldn't do anything on her own outside the home.

This was because she had an old, shabby wheelchair that had tyres that needed pumping up at least once a week. It was worn and it hurt her hands to just push it on flat ground. When the air went out of her tyres she couldn't get up slopes at all.

And she was ashamed of it. It made her feel bad about herself. It also meant that every time she went out she had to have a carer with her to push the wheelchair.

'They think I can't talk!'

Mandy hated this. Because people wouldn't talk to Mandy – instead they would talk to the carer. 'What does she want then?' they would say, or 'Mandy is looking good today, isn't she?' As if Mandy couldn't talk.

People weren't being cruel. Really. But they never properly saw Mandy – because she was stuck in this shabby old wheelchair and everyone felt sorry for her.

They probably thought that Mandy felt as bad as the wheelchair looked. So they thought Mandy couldn't – or didn't want to – speak for herself.

Mandy was angry about this. She wanted a new wheelchair. She wanted an electric-powered wheelchair she could drive by herself so that people could see she was in charge. She was her own person. She could speak for herself!

She didn't mind her carer. In fact she liked her. But she wanted to be seen for herself, for who SHE was – a REAL PERSON!

But the people in charge of giving out wheelchairs said that she couldn't have one. At first they argued that she didn't need a new wheelchair of any kind.

Mandy's care workers said she did need one. Mandy's social worker said it would be nice – but not essential. Mandy said it WAS essential.

So most people agreed that it would be very good for Mandy to have an electric wheelchair. 'But you can't have an electric wheelchair,' they said. 'We can't afford it.'

Mandy had an advocate. Mandy explained to the advocate what was happening.

The advocate didn't know what was the right thing to do. The advocate knew that Mandy really needed this wheelchair, but didn't know whether Mandy had a RIGHT to have an electric wheelchair. The advocate didn't know the law. So the advocate said to Mandy, 'Let's go out together and find out.'

So Mandy and the advocate went to lots of places together. They looked up laws and things on the internet. Everything they read on the internet said that Mandy had a right to an electric wheelchair. An electric wheelchair was a NEED so that Mandy could be independent. That's what the law said.

They went to a Citizens' Advice Bureau and a community law firm. They said that the law was clear that Mandy had to be properly assessed. They both thought that Mandy could show a need for an electric wheelchair.

They spoke to a local councillor – they even spoke to Mandy's MP.

They got a lot of information. They also got a lot of support. They took all this information back to the service provider. They asked for an assessment of Mandy's need.

The assessment said that Mandy had a need for an electric wheelchair. But Mandy was again told there wasn't one available.

The advocate helped Mandy write a letter to the head of the people who paid for her services. Mandy included lots of papers that said she needed a proper wheelchair.

After a lot of meetings, Mandy eventually got her wheelchair.

Mandy also understood more about her rights under the law. She became a good self-advocate. Now she helps advocate for others. This all happened because the advocate and Mandy found out things together.

So you see...
knowing what your rights are under the law is important. Knowing what your advocacy partner's rights are is important. But you don't need to be an expert on the law. You just need to know where to go to find an expert who can help you. Who can advise you.

9. Conclusion

Well, that's it! You should now have all the information you need to become a good advocate. For yourself. And for others.

Just remember – advocacy works best when both the advocate and the partner have support. Like Speaking Up groups. Or belonging to an advocacy or self-advocacy organisation. You can't do everything on your own.

You will always need help finding out things. Sometimes you might need equipment or materials you can't afford. Like a computer or a printer.

If you are part of an organisation or a group, you will find that you can share things that you need. You will find there will always be someone who can help you understand things or find out things with you. You will find there will be people who can support you if you are uncertain about something – or feel like giving up.

So look around and try and find a group that you can join and feel comfortable with. And if there isn't a group in your area that you feel comfortable with – Well, you can always... START ONE OF YOUR OWN!!

GOOD LUCK!

'Nau te rourou naku te rourou kia ora te iwi.'
(With my food basket and your food basket
our guests will be sustained.)
Maori proverb

Ara Tukutuku

Being an advocate is a bit like being a hero. Good advocacy is a story worth telling so that others can learn to be heroes in their own story.

If you have enjoyed the books of speaking up and want to know more, there is a Powerpoint presentation you can watch – it's free! It tells you a little bit more about how the advocacy model works.

You can download Ara Tukutuku from the website of the people who wrote and illustrated the **four books of speaking up**:

www.advocacynetwork.org

We hope you watch and enjoy this Powerpoint presentation.